Journeys from My Pen
To Your Heart

Journeys from My Pen To Your Heart

Carol S. Duncan

iUniverse, Inc.
New York Bloomington

Journeys from My Pen To Your Heart

Copyright © 2009 by Carol S. Duncan

iUniverse books may be ordered through booksellers or by contacting:

iUniverse
1663 Liberty Drive
Bloomington, IN 47403
www.iuniverse.com
1-800-Authors (1-800-288-4677)

Because of the dynamic nature of the Internet, any Web addresses or links contained in this book may have changed since publication and may no longer be valid. The views expressed in this work are solely those of the author and do not necessarily reflect the views of the publisher, and the publisher hereby disclaims any responsibility for them.

ISBN: 978-1-4401-7862-7 (sc)
ISBN: 978-1-4401-7863-4 (ebook)
ISBN: 978-1-4401-7864-1 (dj)

Printed in the United States of America

iUniverse rev. date: 10/19/2009

Kudos to my sweet hubby, Patrick—my soul mate and ever my partner in crime—for his countless hours of proofing my typos and offering valuable insights along the way. Truly, his patience, wisdom, and great sense of humor have all contributed to making my dream a reality.

Contents

Introduction

Stay Awhile

Welcome to my world.
Come on in
And stay awhile.

There's a chair
Beside the window
Waiting just for you
By the fire
Where you'll be warm.

Take your time with every page
Lest you miss a line or two.
Take a journey in your mind
That's all I ask of you.
You may laugh or you may cry…
Sometimes you may even
Wonder why.

If you do, I've done my part
Reaching deep inside my heart,
So welcome to my world.
I'm so glad you came my way.

You can come back any time…
The love will never go away.

2009

Childhood Memories

A Simple Life

The water drips steadily
Into the sink,
Making little if any
Significant noise.

It makes a puddle
Like the rain used to make
When I was a child
And each drop
Was a toy soldier
Marching off to war.

When I was a child,
Life was simple.
All it took to make me happy
Was one black teddy bear,
And how we did dream together.

I cry for the days long gone …
To be suspended there forever.
But life goes on, and we find
It's only what we make it.

Give love freely,
And grasp all that you can in return,
For everyone needs love to grow …

Yet give of yourself completely,
And ask nothing in return,
For everyone needs a lover.

Live life to its fullest,
And think of those
You hold most dear,
For they are your treasures
To walk with through eternity.

The water still drips slowly on,
Telling me life can still be simple.

1978

Take Me Back

I should paint at least one pretty picture
Before I lay my pen back on the shelf,
Like the warmth from the fire
And the smell of Sunday chicken
Frying on the stove.

Take me back to yesterday
When life was young and innocent:
Long rides in the country
On a sunny day
Or quiet naps on a Sunday afternoon.

Days long gone
But remembered
As we sit in the winter of life,
Reminiscing,
Always remembering the good.

Once again,
Take me back to yesterday,
And let me stay there awhile
Among the apple trees on the creek bank,
The places long gone now.

And when life is done,
Let me rest in peace
Among the willows
On the riverbank
I knew as a child.

1980

All-day Sings

At times I wish I could return
To the many Sunday all-day sings
At the little country, black church
Not far from where I was born.

Oh, there was food—
A feast indeed—
And singing and shouting
And occasionally we'd gather
On the riverbanks for a
Baptism in the muddy waters.

And all the while the singing
Continued and all God's children
Got along …

The black, the white,
And whoever came along.

I was just a child,
But those Sunday gatherings
Hold memories most dear.

Today I'm saddened to think
It's not possible.

At times I wonder if
That little country black church
Still has all-day sings.

1980

Seasons of My Life

I was born late *spring* down in the country
In a little house beside some willow trees.
Down the road we'd go fishing by the river
When I was old enough to crawl on papa's knee,
And on down the road always the cows would be grazing
And the crops would be ripening on the vine.
That's the way it was in my childhood memories
Of that old springtime country home of mine.

Summertime was just around the corner.
Pa went and packed the biggest truck I'd ever seen
For our trip north up to the big city.
Pa said for a life with better things.
But I missed the cattle in the pasture grazing,
And the crops all seemed to come straight from cans.
And there's not too much I can remember about summer
In that new city home of mine.

Autumn of my life was soon upon me.
I was mellowed in the concrete atmosphere.
Miles and miles of freeway clogged the big city,
And all the big trees one by one just disappeared,
And the smog covered up all the blue skies,
And all around there were rejects drinking wine,
And that's the way it is in the autumn of my years
In that old rundown city home of mine.

It won't be long now before I reach my *winter,*
And I'm longing to go back to my country home,
Where my roots are still fishing by the river
Even though I'm old enough to stand alone.
I long for the quiet of the peaceful valley,
With memories of life's long-forgotten days.
Oh, take me back and let me spend the winter of my life
In that old springtime country home of mine.

1980

Muddy Waters

Lying stretched out before us,
The creek bed lies,
Undisturbed,
With only occasional
Movement
From nature's intended
Inhabitants.

All clear and inviting as spring,
We invade the tranquility
Momentarily,
Slowly making our way
Upstream,
While behind us
We turn to see the muddy waters
Left in our wake.

And as we travel on,
The realization
That life's pretty much the same
Sinks in.

1981

The Mariner

He said he was
A mariner,
Had sailed more seas
Than I was old,

Which at the time
Seemed to make him
Ancient in my
Young mind.

And oh the yarns
He did spin
Captivated many an hour,

Stimulating the imagination
'Til times I felt
I was sailing the seas with him.

And, even now
That I am older than he was then,
Those tales remain.

And that makes me
Feel young again.

1989

Saturday Pies

Old Mrs. Brown
Didn't make her
Usual apple pie
Last Saturday.

Since the rhubarb
Was fresh and plenty,
She made two of them.
"For a change," she said.

Being a child then,
I didn't understand
Her simple country ways,
Nor the pride she had
In the way she did things.

Of course
She's been gone now
A long time.
But her Saturday pies
Remain a warm memory,

Especially now
That I understand.

1989

Moving On

We lived on the banks
Of the Chattahoochee river
When I was born.

From early days,
We'd fish from those banks,
Having dug the worms
Fresh before going.

I caught one fish
When I was five.

I cried …

So Dad took it
Off the hook.
I kissed it
And threw it back in.

Besides,
He was too small
To keep anyway.

I climbed many a tree then.
Ate those green apples too,
But by now I had
A kindergarten diploma
And was going on *six*.

And that's when we left for the city,

Which was probably the best thing
For the countless worms,

Not to mention the fish.

1989

"And Jigs Made 7 ...."

Dad's church
Was far away in the country
When I was a child.
Nestled back among the pines,
It stood on a hill.
Its outhouses,
That seemed at the time
A great distance
Beyond in the woods,
Also speak of its age
And mine.

One particular winter Sunday,
I recall vividly from memory
How it snowed so hard and deep
And froze us in with no heat.
But the trip we made,
Slowly, just the same.
Dad, because he was the preacher,
Mother, my brother, and me.

And on arriving, we found
The Sunday school superintendent and his wife
Had walked the few blocks there,
Along with their big mongrel dog,
Who was almost the size of a horse
And colored like paint spilled
From all the buckets at once.
And there we were
The total sum on that Sunday.

Dad wrote down *six* in his record book
But added this timely footnote:

"And Jigs made 7 …."

1989

The Goat Story

Dad had another country church
When I was small,
With two outhouses—
His and hers to be exact—
On the other side of the
Little hillside graveyard.

Those were Sundays
We spent the day
Shuffled among the parish folk
Who treated us like royalty,
Spreading a feast fit for kings.

On one particular Sunday
On a hot summer day,
We went to the barn
And milked a goat
For milk to drink with lunch.

Those were simple days
And simple ways,
Nonexistent now

Except in memory.

1979

Father's Day 1949

The sun was just rising.
Mom was busy in her garden
With her roses to adorn
The church alter for the
Special Father's Day service,

While Dad was dressing
My three-year-old brother
In his Sunday best,
When unexpectedly, within
The next thirty minutes,
I came into the world

In the little white house
That subbed as a hospital,
Across the railroad tracks
In the small country town,

Swelling the population
To a whopping sixty-five!

Now the years have passed, and
I just woke up to a beautiful
Sunny day,
But it's a little bittersweet
As I trim the roses
In my garden on this Father's Day,
For both Mom and Dad are long gone.

But I recall their memories
Of what this world was like
On the day my life began.

2005

The Button Jar

When I was but a little girl,
I'd play outside all day long,
And even when the sun did set,
I'd play on and on.

Barefoot, running in the sand,
Nothing stopped my childish plans
Until the rains came,

'Twas all that kept me in.

And those were the days my mother
Took down her *Button Jar*
And let me play with all the
Treasures there within.

What a delight it was
To hold each one
And make up stories grand.

Wish I still had that
Button Jar today.

2007

Kaleidoscopes

Tempo

Like a thousand drums
Beating a steady cadence
In perfect harmony,
Down the tracks
That caught a glimpse
Of the mind's vast canyon
As it went slowly by.

It beat …
Soft …
Then loud,
And all of a sudden
Struck a fear and cry of dismay,
And then as abrupt as it came …
It was gone

Like a thousand soldiers
Marching on the plain,
All in perfect step.
Like the rivers of the mind,
It came slowly …

It went like the dawn ….

That's when sleep came.

1968

When I Think of You

When I think of you,
I see roses in the spring,
A field of yellow daffodils,
A cool mountain stream.

I see a peaceful valley
Beside a waterfall,
A meadow and a babbling brook,
And trees that stand so tall.

I see a heart of gold
With beauty beyond compare,
Gentleness in your being,
As sweet as the morning air.

I see a hidden valley
Where there is no strife,
For when I think of you,
All I see is life.

1979

Words!

Words!

How they flow through my mind
Like a symphony,

From the rich fullness
Of a Stradivarius
To the thundering bellows
Of percussion,

From the flowing soft vibrations
Of Mendelssohn,
To the roaring finale of
"The William Tell Overture."

Words!

How they flow so gently
From my pen
As my heart transposes
All reasoning in my mind

And I convey the warmth I feel
When my thoughts should turn to you.

1979

Kudzu

Memories grow like kudzu
So the past always looks green,
Or should I say greener?

Uncanny though it may seem,
Truth was never truer
And everyday
Memories grow fonder,
And there's no stopping,

For pruning only makes them longer …
As time has become without you

Dear sweet memories.
Like vines tangled in my heart
And mind …

Yet time moves faster than kudzu,
Yet really in the same way.

1979

Out of Reach

Butterflies and flowers are free
For their beauty;

Oceans and rivers are free
As the rain that makes them;

Mountains and deserts are free
For the wayward to conquer and claim;

It seems the best things in life are free.

It's too bad your price tag for love
Is too high and puts you out of reach.

1980

Simple Ability

I'd like to visit the Swiss Alps,
All covered in fresh snow,
And be able to ski the slopes with grace,
Like I was born with skis on both feet.

I'd like to visit Holland:
Watch the windmills turning,
Gather tulips,
And buy a pair of wooden shoes.

I'd like to visit England:
See the changing of the guard,
Perhaps have tea with the Queen,
And read my poetry in royal court.

Don't think me insane,
But I can do all those things,
For I have within the confines of my being
The simple ability to dream.

1980

It Takes Time

It takes time
        To shape the form
                That's resting
On an anvil.

It takes time
        To mold the clay
In the potter's hands.

It takes time
        To write a song
                That's playing
In your mind.

It takes time
        To build a ship
                And a canvas
For a circus tent.

It's no wonder then
        That it just takes time
                For dreams
To come true.

1981

Crackers

"I'd like crackers in my soup,"
I heard the old man say.
"Crackers make it seem to go
A long, long way."

Then with a trembling hand.
He lay down his last dime,
Saying, "Being by the fire
Sure feels fine."

Would you mind if I stay awhile?
I've such a long way to go home,
And once I get there,
I'd just be all alone.

The rain has chilled me to the bone."
He murmured with a sigh,
"The good hot soup will surely
Help me dry."

Later I saw him fumble
With his hat and coat again,
Then said, "I'll be going on my way."
And out the door he went,

Stumbling with his cane
As he walked off in the rain.

1982

Thoughts and Time

I'd like to share
    A thought or two
        To say what's on my mind.

It's really very simple,
    But I never seem to have the time
        That it would take to do so.

So let me put it simply:
    I've tried,
        And what I find is

Trying to say I love you
    Is like trying to catch the wind.

1988

If Only

If only words
    Had wings
        To soar to heights
Above human reach

And yet remain
    Buried deep
        In lovers' souls,

Words would not need
    Be spoken
        To be understood.

1988

Butterflies

Have you ever seen
A multicolored butterfly
Spread its wings
Right before your eyes,

Just like he was doing so
On purpose
To tease you
Before he flies away,
Never to be seen again?

Then you must have noticed
No two are ever the same.

And so it is with us,

For how uniquely different
Are the characters of man.

1988

Thoughts

I should write a book
And call it *Thoughts*
For all the times
I think of things
I want to say
Yet can't.

Just small short entries
Of momentary feelings
That come and go,
And no one knows
The countless times they do.

Just a simple little book
With simple little thoughts
From a complex being
That wishes life was simple.

Yet that's another thought …

1988

Inspiration

In the beginning,
Thoughts transpire,

Stimulated by feelings,
Nourished by love,

Motivated to action,
Thereby creating
Innumerable responses

Captured handsomely
Through various forms
Of artistic flame.

1988

Memories

Throughout the span
Of life

Man accumulates
A reservoir

Of those extraordinary moments
Making his consciousness rich

And from this fullness
Draws them out

As necessity requires

1988

Love Never Takes a Holiday

When I
First noticed
The change in my heart

That love
Had moved in to stay

I didn't know how rich
And full a life could be

But I learned from love
So many things

It made me sing

I spread my wings and found

That love
Never takes a holiday

1988

Justice

The lady holds
Within her hands
Two scales.

When equal
They balance

A system of justice
And fairness for all

But too many times
The scales are tipped
Or are one-sided

And justice
Is really injustice

And we call ourselves free

But for all the greed
Disguised as good
Man is still slave

While the lady
Wears a blindfold

1989

Words on Paper

Words on paper can't begin
To tell you my story

Flowing just like a river
Bending and twisting

But they never come to end
And you have to read them over

Catch the ones
You missed before

And read between
The lines to understand

Those words written on paper
Will never begin to show

All the love buried
Within my heart for you

1989

Looking Back

Looking back in the wake
Of four decades of life,

I'm surrounded by ghosts
That haunt me from dreams
That died along the way.

As the curtain is slowly rising
In the dawning of a new decade,
There are dreams yet to be born.

How strange it seems to be
That life has not even begun

Though half spent getting there.

1989

Night Sounds

Crickets singing
In unison,
Loudly protesting
Sleep,

Are joined by
Countless tree frogs
Adding harmony,

As the wise old owl
Hoots along
All through the night,

'Til one by one,
The birds do sing
A pleasant melody,
Waking the sun of day,

Yet by afternoon,
Everyone naps
For just a little while

As the forest prepares
Another symphony.

1989

Windows

Windows in my heart
Open up sometimes

If only for
A fleeting moment

On the outside
Looking in

You must be
Swift to grasp
The opportunity

For rarely
Is such an
Impromptu emotion
Afforded

Though offered
Without reservations

1989

Kaleidoscopes

Kaleidoscopes constantly change shapes
And colors when enhanced by light
That rivals any rainbow.

Herewith also,
You somehow
Electrify surrounding currents,

Recharging the atmosphere
Instantaneously.

Nonetheless, you do so
Expressively.

When I was young,
Oft times I dreamed
Of life and love
Demonstrative of such qualities.

Metamorphosis still transpires,
Effortlessly it would appear,

Rampant at times,

Regardless of insight into the matter
Of life and love.

1989

And Then There's You ...

The old adage
Nothing ventured
Nothing gained
Comes strangely to mind

As I struggle with
Inner feelings that
Sometimes appear wavering
To my so-called
Contentment.

Each day I'm reminded anew
Of changes taking place
That affect my existence,

Making the simple
Obsolete
And complicated.

And then there's you ...

1989

Sailing Ships

Sailing ships
Drifting aimlessly
On vast oceans
Of blue

With no thoughts
Of time,

Content to be
Alone,
Dreaming of
Ports of call

To be explored
Or passed by,

Dependent
On no one

Save the wind.

1989

The Canvas

Did I ever tell you
I was a dreamer?

Always painting
The canvas
With things
That I only
Wished were
Real,

Not telling
Anyone they
Didn't exist
Except in
My mind?

Well I guess
I'll always be
A dreamer.

Only now
I'm painting
From my heart.

1989

Live Life Now

There will be mountains ahead
In the tomorrows yet to be,

Oceans to cross, rivers that bend,
Days that seem to have no end
To them,

Repeats of yesterdays
That have haunting memories
With tears falling in the night,
Unseen.

So strive to live
One moment at a time.

Grasp its beauty as it's born.
Don't miss the simple things,

For if we worry about what is to be
Or the things already done,

We'll miss the most important
Thing of all …

The life we're living now.

1992

Dreams

Dreams
Are for dreamers,
Just like you and me,
For there's so many things
We really want to do.

Love
Is for lovers,
A bridge that's built
From dreams.

Hand in hand
We walk along
Life's shores,
Over shifting sands.

Night
Comes for dreaming.

It is the tie that binds
Dreams of lovers into one.

1993

Shoelaces

There was a time
Life was simple,

When the hardest thing
Was mastering shoelaces,

In the land
Of sweet innocence

Before the age
Of accountability
Fashioned the difference
Between right and wrong.

Days were carefree then.

There was no hatred
In young hearts,

Bias posed no threats
To dreams and ambitions
Of becoming all
There was to be.

Times are not so
Simple now.

Innocence gave way
To belated wisdom
Through many
A joyful and bitter
Tear

While tripping
On untied shoelaces.

1993

My Quiet Place

The truth is,

For some obscure reason,

I cannot begin to remember
The last time I visited
My quiet place.

It's where I go to contemplate
Life with its mysteries:

A place to be still and listen
To those innermost thoughts
That get shoved in a corner,
Then into small crevices to boot;

A place I reflect—remember—
All the happy, all the sad,
All the good, all the bad

To be reborn with a fresh outlook
Clearing the cobwebs in my mind.

I feel a need to travel back again
To that quiet place
And while away the hours
For just a little bit

And take a short break
From the merry-go-round of life.

2005

Inhale

In the early dawn
Walking among the roses
I'm astounded.

The dew forms
On intricate petals

And glistens in the
First rays of the sun
That is soon to rise
And beat down overhead.

Soon the aroma

That certain fragrance

Will reach the senses
And I'll inhale the moment
And register it
In my mind for later use.

The roses' deep-red color
Reflects in your eyes
When I look there

And makes me smile.

2006

Poems

In my youth
Lines were short

Words were few
But thoughts were many.

Now that I am old
Lines are long

Words are many
And thoughts are endless.

Such are the poems of life.

2006

Solitude

My mind wanders
Through graduated sequences

Each a little deeper into thoughts
As I'm momentarily
Bound in solitude

Sweet precious time
That is allotted
For such a variation of life

And it's quiet—almost too quiet
To hear myself think out loud

For I can hear the beating of my heart
That says I'm alive in here

And if I close my eyes
I'll find you there—as always

2006

Always

I am truly convinced
In my heart of hearts
That you know my wish for you
Is sunshine and roses everyday

And for nothing but good things
To come your way
No matter the circumstances.

If life were just that simple
What a better place
This old world would be.

So the trick is to simply think
Good things always,

Love the ones you love
Even more than you already do,

And be thankful for all in life
That comes your way.

2008

Indwelling

What lover hasn't reveled
Strolling hand in hand
Beside the ocean fair?

Nary a one.

For all who venture
This way
Have an indwelling
Romanticism already

That spurs tons
Of verbiage
To the poets of old

And speaks of love
Like the mighty ocean
That rolls on and on

For its beginnings
Have no ends.

2006

The Flowers

I'm not sure just what it was
That caught my attention
Through the corner of my eye,

Stopping me in my tracks,
Dead still, silent,
Staring in awe.

Was it the blood-red vase
That held the delicate arrangement
Of white carnations, white daises,
And white roses?

Or that stargazer lily
With its striking red stripe
That made it stand so tall?

So simple yet so eloquently
That one could surely feel
The obvious love coming from
The sender and receiver in turn
That left me breathless for a moment,

However with a smile.

2006

Dare to Go

Beneath the towering
Thundering waterfall
Lays a pool

So serene
Deep and inviting

Dare to go beyond
The labyrinth of caves
And mazes

And come to the other side
Where only few ever go
And you'll find a land of plenty

A meadow and a shire

All your heart could ever long for
And more

You'll never know
What's beyond that gate

Unless you take that leap
And dare to dream while you're awake.

2007

Complete

Teddy bears
And county fairs
Are childhood memories.

Hide and seek,
Now don't you peek,
An era so far gone.

The sun goes down,
The cows come home,
It's a way of life.

Up at dawn,
You carry on,
That's just
How it should be.

But loving you
Is a different thing.
It makes my life
So sweet.

For loving you
Is the thing I find
That makes my life
Complete.

2007

Carry Me Home

Drifting slowly upon the water,
The sunshine beating down,
I keep waiting for the wind
To carry me home.

The sails set high,
But with no breeze
To blow them
They're just my shelter
From the sun.

Won't nature give me the wind
To carry me home?

She's fickle,
Just like a lover,
But she'll come in her own good time.

'Til then I'll sail aimlessly along
'Til the wind comes
To carry me home.

I need the wind behind my sail
To carry me home.

2007

The Magic Within
for B.J.O.

Today the sky is blue and the sun is shining,
Yet they say it may turn gray and rain
Before the day is through.

You see …

You'll come to understand
Life is a bit like the weather:
Unpredictable no matter how hard
You try to plan for it.

This old world is full of wars.
Sorrow and hatred run amok,
Yet there is love for the taking,

And you will be born into love,
For love is what brought you here.

So as the golden sands drop through
The hourglass that is the
Time we are allotted,

My wish for you is happiness,
Joy, and love

Measured in equal sums,
Just like the magic within.

For all the world's problems
Went directly to the back burner
And disappeared the moment you arrived
And captured our hearts.

2007

Facets of Love

Who Could Ask for More?

I was awakened the previous night to the sound
Of winter's rain mixed with sleet and snow.
As the wind whistled through the tiny cracks

In my window, the cat lay contentedly
Purring at the foot of my bed,
Perhaps unaware that as he slept
In the warmth of the burning cinders
Of the evening fire, a blanket of white
Covered the earth just outside.
I had a chance to walk in it,

Though it wasn't very deep,
And there in the glistening snow gathered
A dozen or so pecans latent from last summer's
Crop, which had been hurled there
From the now bare branches during the storm.

I lay and listened awhile to the peaceful sounds
That surrounded me and felt content
And at peace with my maker,

For indeed He gave me eyes to see,
Ears to hear, life to live,
And you to love.

Who could ask for anything more?

1979

Just between You and Me

I stepped from the room

Briefly,

Not really long enough
To bat an eye,

Yet when I returned,
I felt a chill
Go up and down my spine
As if something was amiss.

I looked around
And you were gone,

And all you left behind
Was a half-smoked cigarette
That still smoldered

And a glass of ice water
In which the cubes had melted,
Leaving a warm and funny taste.

Oh

I knew today was coming,
And I had no doubt it would,

Yet I felt a little saddened,
Like a child when he
Breaks his favorite toy.

And though there were no tears,
I felt like I could cry,

For you walked off in the rain,
And you didn't say good-bye.

1979

Engulfed

I turned over
In my sleepless dreams
And reached for you,
But you weren't there.

I lay a long time
Just staring into
The illusionary emptiness
Surrounding me,

Feeling a bitter cold chill
Engulfing my being
In the darkness
As my nose sensed the sweaty
Anger and frustration building inside,

Sounding as a deep roar
On a stormy night.

I listened to the music
But couldn't recall the lyrics,
So I hummed along, half asleep,

'Til once again
Dreams carried me away in the night.

But when morning came,
I awoke to find
It wasn't a dream.

I reached for you,
But you were gone.

God,
What a lonely feeling.

1979

I Thought of You

I turned over from my sleepless dreams,
Listening to the drizzling rain
Falling softly on the new green grass
Through my window.

The sky seemed to be weaved
In black and gray,
With no hope of the sun,
Then I thought of you.

I closed my eyes and you were there,
Touching close.

I reached out and our minds were one.

Busily I went about the morning
Filling each waking moment
With thoughts of you.

And though you're not far away,
It's only a small thought
That brings you close.

And as I hurry to meet the day,
The wet, the cold, the bitter day,
I felt warm, content, and loved.

For I thought of you
And smiled.

1979

Once Loved

I used to think of us as one

Inseparable

Walking hand in hand together
Down the streets of yesterday

How we laughed
And time stood still
And we shared and we loved
And the skies were blue

Then one sweet day
The skies turned gray
And the wave of the storm swallowed us

And you and I were swept away
To different worlds
'Til we reached the now tomorrow

Now you're just another color
On my rainbow of lost loves

Inseparable

1979

Just Me

If I were but the master of words
Instead of lines
I would tell you what lies deep.

If I had the gifted voice of song
I would compose a melody
To sing just for you.

But I am only me
Without the ability of words
To speak

Nor the gift of voice
With which to sing.

All I know is I love you
And nothing will ever be the same.

1980

Beckoning

I hear the ocean beckoning,
Singing my name with each wave
It sends rushing to the shores
To die a needless demise.

Yet from the bottom of its depths
It coughs up the next heaving breath
That sends white foam
Hurdling and racing,
Trying to catch the one before,

Sometimes overtaking
As the two become one,
Wed momentarily to the same vow—
'Til death do us part.

Still, each rippling wave
Sings my name with desire and longing.

For each breath you take heaves a sigh,
For you are the ocean,
And I am the land

And we can only meet
Momentarily on the shore.

1980

Wild Goose Chase

I've just returned from another
Fanciful wild goose chase
Searching for the nonexistent you.

At times it infuriates me
To the point of desolation,

And then times again
I conceive notions to follow the wind

As I have a repertoire of endless dreams
To be acted out in installments.

So off tomorrow I'll go
Looking for you again,

But I wonder what I'd do
If ever I found you.

1980

I've Got You

In this world from day to day
We go about life unknowing.
We just never stop to see
All the things that are free.
We just take for granted
The sun will rise tomorrow,
But we never take the time
To let others just be.

If we live from day to day
And go about life knowing,
Taking time to stop and see
All the things that are free
But never take for granted
We'll live 'til tomorrow,
Maybe then we'll find the time
For others to be.

Meadows have green grass,
Summer storms have rainbows,
Puppy dogs have wagging tails,
Little children have dreams,
Springtime has roses,
Winter storms have snow,
Everyone has something,
And I've got you.

Everyone loves something,
And I love you.

1980

Search Unending

My search for words
It never ends

For the songs
Never quit coming
In my mind

And all the time I write
I'm writing more in my mind
That I never get on paper

But as long as I live
I'll dream on
And sing inside my soul

For never does the music
Seem to end

Even in peaceful sleep
My mind thirsts for still
New ways to say I love you

1981

Changing

Changing

Every breath of life
Is different
From the one before.

Each hour makes us
Older as they turn
Into days and nights,
Forgotten as
The seasons come
And go.

So how can you say
You know me
When I don't
Know myself?

How can one
Ever really
Be the same after love?

1989

Love's Not Finished

I wasn't looking
Anymore

Thought the time
For love had passed me by

Sadly I closed the door
On dreams that
Were never meant to be

Then suddenly
Out of the sky
You landed in the middle
Of my heart

Unexpected as could be

And I find now
That love's not quite finished
Yet in me

1989

Yes

It seems
I've lost my mind

And reasoning
Isn't any good
To answer
The questions
Jumbled there

But you see

You stole my heart
And that makes
Me laugh

And feel
Funny inside

Is that what love is?

1989

Life Became a Holiday

I don't need a rhyme
Nor reason
To say I love you

Or tell you
How I feel inside,

For all my love
Shows through.
For whenever you look
In my eyes,
You can see it there,

Hear it in the echoes
Of my laughter everywhere.

No

It doesn't take a special day
To make me feel this way,

For my life became a holiday
On the day I met you.

1991

Essence of You

Slowly
I have become you

Cemented through
The love
That bonds us
Together as one

All the parts
Of me
Now have melted
And fused

Making my existence
The very essence
That is you.

1991

Affaire du Coeur

Guess you could say it's just
An affaire du coeur,
For I have no mind to reason
When it comes to loving you,

And no one could ever tell me
That I was wrong to feel
The way I do,
For no one knows my heart
Better than me.

So I guess it's really
Safe to say
A love like ours is best this way
When it's coming from
And shared just by one.

Maybe it's crazy, but it's true:

The secret to happiness
Is right before our eyes

When love is
An affair of the heart

1991

Within

Thoughts of you
Fill every minute crevice
Of my being

And I'm warmed
By the love
Burning deep
Within my heart
That comes from you

And thus being there

You're with me
Every step I take

Every hour
Of every day
And passing night

Making me smile
From your abundance
Within

1992

Never Ending Love

It's rhapsody, harmony,

Sweet music in your soul
When you find the one you'll love
And cherish all your life.

There'll be tears
From joy and laughter
Springing from happiness within.

You'll shout it from the rooftops,
Echoes blowing in the wind,

Yet it's pristine,

Pure as the first fallen snow
And gentle too,
Like snowflakes fall.

Two become just one,
A blanket that covers
A multitude of various aspects
That is life.

Only love such as this
Knows no bounds
And is never ending.

2006

Across the Room

I see you standing there
Clear across the room,

See you turn your head
And smile a smile
I know that's meant for me.

I gaze into your eyes,
But is that really wise?

For I lose all my senses,
All of my control,
For I'm captured by your smile

That lets me know
You feel the same.

And no words need to pass
Or exchange.

It's all registered
In your eyes.

And as my heart
Skips a beat,

I can almost feel
The warmth
Of your hand in mine

Clear across the room.

2006

You Define My Love

I awoke again last night.
It was the middle of the night.

Woke to find you there beside me
And I had to smile.

The moon crept into the room.
Its beams danced across your face,
And I could almost trace the outline
Of a smile that rested there.

I wake up almost every night
Just to watch you sleep,

Trying to find another way
To say what's deep inside,

Like "You're the sum
Of all my dreams,
My rock, my guiding light."

And I've tried so many ways
To tell you,

Oh so many times,

But suffice it now
Just to say,

"You define my love."

2006

If Thoughts Had Wings

If thoughts had wings
Like birds that fly,

They would carry wishes
Straight from my heart

Across the expanse of time
And land safely in yours.

Then you'd know these were
My thoughts for you today.

Just picture yourself

Holding hands with the one you love,

Watching the sunset across the ocean

Or snow falling and gently covering the ground

Or seeing the sunrise slowly peeking through the trees

Or just enjoying a rainbow after the storm

And then there's apple pie, ice cream

Root beer floats, parades and balloons,

Teddy bears, country fairs, catching fire flies,

Late summer nights running barefoot
In the park, and roses.

But most of all, I wish for you
Peace that passeth all understanding,

The strength to carry on,

And to always remember,
No matter what,

Love conquers all.

2006

The Unexpected

It's as if you stepped out of a cloud
Straight into my heart
When I least expected and needed someone
Or something to believe in.

It took me by surprise,
For your beauty took my breath away,
And my subconscious had to remind me
To breathe again
As I stood in awe,
Thinking you were only a dream

Until you touched my hand
And love flowed through my veins
In rapid succession.

Your smile captivated my soul,
Swallowing it whole,
'Til I was consumed by you.

Now I can't imagine
Even one single day of my life
Without you in it.

2006

Wings of Love

There are so many songs
My heart longs just
To sing to you

A luring melody
To make you come away
And if I could have my wish

It would simply be just this
Come ride the wind
On wings of love with me

And we'll soar
To heights unknown
Where we've never been before

Glide along the sunset on the shore
Resting in the shadows
Of evening tide

Safely sailing with the wind
On wings of love

2006

Convoluted Love

Ever since the dawn of time,
Man has tried to define
That elusive phenomenon
We call love.

And for centuries,
Man has drawn conclusions
On walls, on paper,
In books

And never has captured
The whole of the matter,
Notwithstanding love being
The convoluted mistress in us all.

So for ages yet to be,
Man will still be baffled
And fooled at the existence
Of this remarkable entity

To which there is
Neither a right nor a wrong answer.

2006

Now

Wish I could find a way
To turn back the time
Knowing what I know now
And have you for mine

But life never works out
Quite that way

How I missed those years
Without you here

But in the autumn of my life
I have you now and it's
All that matters anyhow
For we can't change the time

We can't just rewind
The days we lost
Before we were found

So I'll love you more
With a love that's deep
And has no shame

It's my gift to you
Love forever true

2006

That's the Way

Love makes you weep; it makes you cry;
It makes you laugh; it leaves you high
As it comes and goes like the river flows.
That's the way love grows.

Love makes you sad when raindrops fall.
It makes you glad for sunny skies.
Like the seasons change, we can't rearrange.
That's the way love grows.

Love is all the things you want it to be,
All your heart could ever long for and more,
When you finally realize
That it's right before your eyes
And your heart knows it's for sure.
That's the way love grows.

When your heart knows it's for sure,
That's the way love grows.

2006

Tell Me

Tell me where is it infinity ends
And eternity begins?

Tell me where does the ocean
Go to sleep at night?

How high can eagles fly?

Tell me what is in your heart
'Cause mine is just aching to know.

Give me words to say you'll understand
When they reach your ears,
That will make you feel the love
I have for you.

Tell me how can the sun rise and fall
Or a rainbow fill the sky?

Tell me what does it take
To make the flowers bloom?

Tell me what's in your heart.

Do you see the stars?

Can you feel the love?

My heart longs to know,

Where does love begin?

2007

It's the Price You Pay

Some say love
Is a fickle thing
That comes and goes
Just like winter into spring.

It can fill you up
Then leave you dry.
It can make you laugh,
Turn and make you cry.

I say love
Is a gentle thing—
A breath of air
Like a slow-falling rain.

It consumes your soul.
It gives you wings.
It will make you sing.
Such is love's refrain.

And your love
Is the sweetest love of all,
So much more
Than words could ever say.

I'd walk through fire
Just to be with you.

That's the price I'd pay.

That's the price you pay.

That's the price of love.

2007

Secrets

Soon the sun will
Be going down
As darkness
Fills the sky,

A perfect cover
Overhead
To hide the million
Tears I've cried.

But my pillow will
Swallow them
And keep
My secrets safe,

So you'll never know
How just the thought of you
Can turn my gray skies blue.

You'll never know
The heart of me
That longs to be with you,

But one day maybe
I'll wake to find
That dreams really
Can come true

And you will love me too.

2007

Moments

There comes a time in everyone's journey
Across this span of life
When the planets are simultaneously
Aligned perfectly
And the world is tilted
On its axis

When here comes that defining moment
That tells us just why, nay
Who we are

Then there are those moments
Held in our subconscious
That contains our memories

The very essence that is us

Yet it is the time I'm with you, my love
In the here and now
That is the most precious

Priceless treasure
Of them all

2008

Lover's Lullaby

When the day is done
Then the evening comes
And the night birds
Seek a lofty perch
In a starry sky
When the moon shines down
You can hear the sound
Of the sweet refrain
Of a lover's lullaby

Since the dawn of time
It has been the same
The quest for love
Makes us act like fools
While we play our games
As the night birds sing
In perfect harmony
I'll sing for you
A lover's lullaby

Summer, autumn
Winter, spring
The seasons move along
Love will never ever die
In the words within a song

When the night is done
When the dawn has come
And the night birds
Fly away until
The set of sun
All through the day
Echoes linger on
Deep inside your heart
From a lover's lullaby

2009

Do You Ever Think of Me?

Do you ever stop to wonder what I do
With all my time when you are gone?
Do you ever stop to ponder all the little things
You've often heard me say?

Do you wonder where the time goes
Or even how the tide flows?
Do you wonder why the flowers
Bloom in spring?

Do you wonder while you're laughing
Why that silly song just makes your heart sing?
Do you think of me like I think of you?

I count the moments when you're gone,
I count each second on the clock,
I count the clouds drifting by,
I count each beat inside my heart,
I count the memories we've made,
I close my eyes, and I see your face.

I think of you; do you think of me?

All through the day when you are gone
I think of you.

Do you ever think of me?

2009

Whimsical

Read Myself

There are times
I go a long time
Without picking
Up my pen

Times I don't
Jot down
The way I feel
Nor the places
I have been

Yet when I do
I put these
In my books
Upon the shelf

There to age

And at times I go
And read myself
To myself

1979

One by One

One by one I write the words
Fill up page after page
'Til my mind runs out of words to say

Like the sun always sets
Or gets devoured by a giant cloud
That spits it out
On the other side of the world

Like it's playing ball back and forth
And that makes night and day

Sometimes I sit and write for you

Sometimes I write you in the past
Sometimes I write you in the future

Sometimes I write you in the present
As if you were here with me

Sometimes I wonder what people would think
If they knew you never really existed at all

1980

Mmmmm ...

Ever notice
How funny it really is
That in winter
We turn up the heat
To escape the cold

Maintaining the temperature
As if it was summer outdoors

Not to leave out the fact
How we cringe
When the heating bills come
Hoping spring's now far behind

And then comes summer

And the heat goes down
And on go the air conditioners
Bringing down the thermostat
Colder than having no heat
In winter

Cringing at the electric bills
Making us wish
Fall would hurry along

1981

Death and Taxes

Two things are certain:

Death and taxes.
Yet they say you must relax.

While things are changing every day,
New taxes I must pay.
Now clearly in my mind I see

Even dying will be a tax on me.

1989

Robins

The robin built her nest
Among my climbing roses,
Right above the trellis,
I found out quite by accident
The other day.

As I was trimming,
She swooped down
And scolded me relentlessly
For disturbing her home.

Since then I've seen her
Come and go
And heard her singing
And wondered if she'd stay.

Yet today I heard
The tiny voices singing
And caught a glimpse
Of one baby bird,
And I smiled.

Needless to say,
Those roses won't
Be trimmed this season.

1989

When I Can't Sleep

It's two o'clock
And I can't sleep.
I even tried
Counting sheep.

I turned and asked
The cat nearby
To close her eyes,
Try counting mice.

Then I laughed
And wondered at
What she thought of that,
My cat.

I mean if we count sheep

When we can't sleep

Does the cat count mice?
Does the dog count cats
Unless he's a bird dog?

I laughed out loud.
'Twas all in fun,
But I'm glad to say
This poem is done!

1989

Wordless

I get wordless
When I try to tell you
I love you

I'm renowned
For lack of words
When I'm with you

I'm just merely
Ordinary

The songs I sing
Never carry the message
Locked inside my heart

I get silly
Bemused and dizzy

Expertly so

When I try
To tell you
I love you

1989

The Toy

It was not so long ago
I was your brand new
Squeaky toy

All polished and bright
Complete with bells and whistles
And oh how the gleam
In your eyes shone

I especially loved the music
In your laughter
As you took me everywhere
You went
And declared your love for me

But didn't I warn you
That breaking me
Would make you cry

Even one shiny knob
Or bell that made me unique
Being gone would make me useless

And now that day has come
And I'm on top of the heap
Of castaways

Only
I have this burning question
I long to ask

Just why is it

If you loved me so

You always slept
With that worn out
Frazzled teddy bear?

2006

A Love Story

A plain white sheet of paper
Beckons me to give it
A purpose to come to life
With words that flow
From the pen in abundance.

It begs me to make it come alive
With those melodious sounds
That speak of love
That might make it
Immortal in the end.

But alas,

The pen is floundering
In the throes of oblivion
And wrestling the ink
That flows freely.

Who knew the pen and paper
Could share so poignant
A love story?

2006

Silliness

Ever notice when you're cold I'm hot?
The two elements collide
When they come together,
Yet complement each other
In different ways.

Then when you're hot I'm cold,
But the universe keeps on
Spinning and spinning
On its axis
And never falls off.

So I wonder

What would really happen if the day
Ever came to find ourselves
Hot or cold simultaneously?

Would the world actually
Stand still
And we cease to be?

Or would we even notice?

2006

Ode to Puppies

So my oldest friend
Calls me the other day
And we chatted
For a long while

Since we haven't
Had a chance to
Catch up lately
With all the things
That have happened
In our lives

And she laughed
And wondered if I still
Used the term *puppies*
For everything.

Oh yeah,

That is my watch word,

My word for everything
When I can't think of
Just what it is
I want to say.

Have I got some puppies for you!

It's just one of my most enduring,
Charming ways of explaining myself.

Ask anyone who knows me.

They'll tell you
What puppies
Are all about!

2006

Hushed Puppy

So my enduring spouse
Says to me at lunch today,

After telling him
About my early rise
And the poems
That came out of it,

That he had
A second idea
For my epitaph:

Simply put—
"Hushed Puppy,"

For he hears my puppies
Referred to so often
He felt it fitting.

Only it won't fit
On any urn,

Hence,
Duct tape it
Before you toss it
Into that big blue ocean
My sweet.

You know,

It's good to laugh.
It helps heal the pain.

2006

One by One by One

When we were much younger,
We'd sit by the ocean tide
And dream of things yet to be.

Those were the days
Of wine and roses
And chocolate covered
Strawberries.

Oh, love was sweet
And innocence abounded.
What love was that?

Years later we come to sit
At ocean's tide
And reminisce,

To gather moments
Of supreme happiness
Just in doing so,

And my love makes me laugh
As he feeds me
Of all the fare that be—

Fritos …

One by one
By one.

2006

Guilty

You told me that you loved me,
So I told you I loved you too.

Now you're judging me, and
You're saying that I'm guilty,
And yes, my love, that's true.

I'm guilty in the first degree
But just for loving you.

So take me to jail,
The verdict is in,
And I've been condemned
Of loving you in the first degree.

So I'll spend my lifetime in your arms,
But you'll be in mine too

'Cause the jury has now spoken,
And you're just as guilty too.

2007

Of Fairy Wings and Rutabagas

On this day
Probably more than any day

Sentiments are being sent
To tell how much love
Exists inside for that
Special someone

For it's a known fact
That no matter
How old one is

A heart that loves
Stays forever young

So once again
A pattern emerges

As letters hold hands
Skipping merrily across
The pages forming words
That go boldly into the arena

And go happily dancing
Onto the stage of life

Transforming thoughts into images
Of fairy wings and rutabagas

2009

Re: Of Fairy Wings and Rutabagas

Although I would be the first to admit
There is no such thing as fairy wings
Since there is no such thing as fairies,
Or is there?

However, I can truthfully say
I abhor those nasty turnips
My dad grew on the south forty;
I really did.

I can foresee one day
Those men in crisp white coats
With their butterfly nets and restraints
Coming for me,
Or did they do that already?

You know there's a fine line
Between imagination and reality,
And I can recall being severely punished
For showing signs of imagination.
The scars ran deep
And covered over during the years,
But did they?

I still write of love
And the way things are in my mind,
For it's a welcoming place I go
When I sit and let myself wonder.

But wouldn't it be funny
If after all is said and done
That the thing people will remember most
When they finish my book

Would be the images
Of fairy wings and rutabagas?

2009

A Pirates Song ... or Simply Put Mateys ... ARRGG!!

Gather 'round lassies and I'll tell ye a tale
Of a handsome young pirate and the seas he did sail.
He claimed every heart in all the ports he did roam,
But he never stayed long, for the sea was his home,
Singing, "Hidey–ho, mateys, my home is the sea.
Hidey–ho, boys, you'll never catch me.
So hide the sweet ladies and sleep while you can
'Cause when that norther' wind blows
You know I'll come back again."

He kissed all the ladies and stole every heart;
In the matters of love this pirate was smart.
He crept through the night, he was fearless and bold,
But all that he really had wanted was gold,
Singing, "Hidey–ho, mateys, my home is the sea.
Hidey–ho, boys, you'll never catch me.
So hide the sweet ladies and sleep while you can
'Cause when that norther' wind blows
You know I'll come back again."

True to his word, he sailed back again and again
'Til they caught him and bound him and threw him in jail.
He hung from the gallows one cold winter's day,
But wouldn't you know he had the last word to say?
He sang, "Hidey–ho, mateys, now I'm one with the sea.
Hidey–ho, boys, now my spirit is free.

You should hide the sweet ladies and sleep if you can
'Cause when that norther' wind blows
You know I'll come back again.
Whenever she blows, I'll sail back again."

2009

Mortality

Mind Metamorphosis

This is my genesis

Long I have waited
To emerge from the plexus
Of the cocoon
That held my embryo captive

I spread my multicolored
Wings to fly
But alas
The winds of time
Are too strong in my newness

I seek shelter from the storm
'Til I rise in flight once more

I searched the valleys and the plains
The snowcapped mountains
And the vast depth of the ocean floor
Looking for myself

I searched the deep canyons
And the minute crevices of my mind
And found my utopia

Once again I rise
To the winds of time
Gently blowing me
Silently along

'Til I meet my Omega

1976

Free Spirit

In the breeze I hear my name
Singing on the wind

And each wave going back on evening tide
Just calls me one time more

The canyons seem to echo
The mountains bid me climb

The time has come to follow
This dream inside my mind

I don't know where it will lead me
If to a near or distant shore

All I know is if I don't follow
It may not call me anymore

1981

After the Storm

God never said that there would not be storms,
He never said the rain would never come,
He never said the stars would always shine,
But He said, "I'll be there through it all."

God never said that there would not be tears,
He never said that heartaches would never come,
He never said that life would all be smiles,
But He said, "I'll be there through it all."

God never said that life would all be roses,
He never said all bodies would be strong,
He never said we all would live like kings,
But He said, "I'll be there through it all."

After the storm, God sends a rainbow,
So look up when life gets you down.
He's waiting there to dry your tears.
He will keep you safe from harm.
Yes, after the storm, God sends a rainbow.

1982

Beyond Roses and Thorns

Beyond roses and thorns
Lies tomorrow
Free from the wants of today
Void of lost loves of yesterday

All peaceful and serene
A hidden valley
Known only to those who live
Through the love of today's roses
And the thorns of yesterday

Lord grant that we should wake
From the peaceful yet restless
Slumber of the night
In a land of tomorrow
Beyond roses and thorns

1988

Stages

One by one
  I fill the pages

Words that are
  The very stages
  Of my life

Thought by thought
  I feel the pages

See the many
  Different stages
  Of my life

Day by day
Each breath I take makes me
  Realize that time's too
  Short now

Got to go now
And feel the pages

Watch the stages

Changing,
  Ever changing

Capture the stages
Of my life

1989

Summer Leigh

From innocence and youth
You never came
But life was full
And time was plenty.

Nonetheless,
Youth faded in the shadows
As the seasons came and went
In rapid succession

Yet in my heart
I dreamed of you
For time was still my ally

And I laughed and said
I'd call you Summer Leigh
If you happened now to come

But fate slipped in
And dealt her blow
And you weren't meant to be

Now youth is gone
And time is gone

The friends I thought once mine
Left me to face
The years of bitterness alone

While the candlewick slowly flickers
And I die wondering why

1989

Dissipate

For all the words I write
There must be thousands
I never do

For all the thoughts I capture
There are countless ones
That dissipate before
They are contained

And maybe dreams
Are the same

Or maybe it's that
As we grow older we see life
In a different mode

And come to accept things
With realism
Letting fantasies go

Tending to make life bittersweet

1989

Summer's Last Red Rose

Today I cut
The last red rose
Of summer

Leaving the bush
Standing bare
Yet triumphant

For fall buds
Soon will blossom

And though summer is done
Its roses all gone

Silently it reminds me
Life goes on

As the old
Makes way
For the new

And that some things
Such as love

Never *ever* die

1989

September's Song

Looking back
On all the yesterdays
That run swiftly through my mind
Sweet memories appear
When I close my eyes to reminisce
And sing September's song.

The leaves of green
Now glow red and gold
In the twilight of the setting sun

The flower blooms have all
Grown and found their way
To vases sitting on tables far away
Now I sing September's song.

The wind slowly blows
An autumn breeze
Past the windowsill
In the early morning hours

As I pull the blanket
Snuggly around my head
I think of how autumn
Fills me with wonder

And how deeply rooted
Is September's song

1995

Retrospect ... for Pa
March 22, 1925–April 13, 2000

Looking back
Over all the years,
They seem so few
Now that you're gone.

The tides of endless tears
Swell but do not follow.

Time stands still
For the moment.
Nothing else seems to matter.

I sort through countless memories.
Even sleep does not evade the issue

As I try to find contentment
In the peace that passeth
All understanding.

And life, well,
It still marches on.

A drummer inside beckons,
However, at a different pace

Since I have seen the face of death
And heard the angels whisper.

2000

Crossroads ... for Ma

February 22, 1925–January 19, 2001

It started out like a dream
From which I never woke
As time marched on

Somehow masking days and nights,
But by then it was all too real.

You slipped away with no fanfare,
No good-byes,

No time to be prepared
For what you can never be anyway.

That was the moment at the crossroads
Where life and death meet
And separate us,

The moment where life ends or begins
All depending on perspective.

So now as winter
Slowly gives way to spring,

Does the heart mend?

2001

Dance with Me Again

Take my hand and come walk with me
Through the paths unknown.

Oh, my love, come dance with me
Where the lilies bloom in the dale.

Climb the mountains to the highest peak
As the dawn begins to break.

Hear the music as the ocean roars
To shore at end of day.

Seasons come and seasons go,
Rain and wind, sun and snow,
Just like the seasons of our lives:

Good and bad, happy, sad.

Come sit with me
When evening shadows dim.

Thinking back on all our memories
Will help to keep us warm.

Oh, my love, come dance with me again.

2005

The Stirring Pot

Inside my mind's eye
Stands a black cast iron cauldron
Sitting on three huge claw feet
Over a roaring flame

Where within all the words and phrases
Are stirring around until
They pour forth into sometimes
Beautiful prose

Making one laugh or cry
Depending on the outcome

Which may be instantaneous
During or at the end

For somehow it reaches in
And grabs and tugs
At heartstrings in different ways

And I must capture all I can
Before the flame is gone

And words no longer have
Rhyme or reason to exist

2005

Time

Oh time,

Sweet innocence of youth,
Where did you go?

Seems like only yesterday
I was running barefoot in the sand
And watching as the waves
Destroyed the castles I built there,

Or running through the open meadow
With my kite, high in the sky,
That disappeared into the clouds
Or sometimes a neighboring tree.

But time,

Where did these white hairs
On my head come from?

Is it really the age of wisdom
I'm thrust upon?

Oh time,

Where did you go?

Better yet,
Where are we going now?

2006

Ode to an Aging Man

'Tis one of life's
Remaining mysteries

Youth's sweet innocence
Suspended in quantum
Sanctuary

Encompassed by
Wondrous revelations
And copious sentiment

But alas,
The boy grows to be a man
In sequence

As time revolves
To yet a higher plane

And yet only found
In repose of remembrance

Unless by chance
In crossing over
Some boy remains in the man

2006

A Brand New Day

When you find yourself alone
At the end of the day
And you feel the walls around you
Start closing in,

Just remember through the sorrow
There is always one more tomorrow
And life is brighter in the dawn
Of a brand new day.

I'll be here to help you
Through the bad times.
I'll be here when you need
A hand to hold.

When things get hard
And you need a shoulder to cry on,
I'll be here with outstretched arms
Waiting for you.

So look now to the light
Of a clear bright morning.
Sing praises now
For the light of a brand new day.

When troubles come,
Just let my love surround you.
Let sorrows die in the light
Of a brand new day.

When troubles come,
Just feel my love surround you.
All sorrows die in the light
Of a brand new day.

2007

Maiden Voyage

I set sail on an early Sunday morning
As dawn was breaking on the horizon
And the dew lay glistening on the roses.

The course lay outstretched ahead,
Still uncharted or unseen.

Depending on which way the
Winds of time would blow
Shaped those paths along the way.

The sands of the hourglass started slowly
Dropping one by one, turning into days.
Then days turned to months,
Months to years, and years to decades,

As time marched steadily forward,
Picking up speed with each step.

I've found beauty in the red and gold leaves
In the autumn of my days,

And I know the reality of the
Cold, dark dismal days of winter are close,

But I'll smile and laugh in the face of death
When I reach the last port of call,
For it was an incredible journey,

This maiden voyage that was life.

2008

Journey

Like a mighty raging river
That rushes swiftly to the shore
And spills out of its confined spaces,
Trickling into a multitude of
Lakes and streams and valley floors,
Love can't be corralled nor contained,
For it's always on the move,
Growing on its journey to be free.

My love for you could fill an ocean
As deep and wide as the day is long,
And sing from its depths
A multitude of love songs
That spring forth from my heart,
That I will write for you
'Til this life comes to an end.

2008

Drifting

Fishing on the river banks
Running barefoot through
The open meadows

Climbing up those apple trees
Chasing fireflies
'Til the sun went down

Lazy Sunday afternoons
The smell of frying chicken
Fills the air

Dragging my teddy bear
Everywhere

But you know I was just a child

Strolling now
Down memory lane
When life was very simple

Now the evening shadows wane
As I am growing old

How have the years
Just passed me by

Tell me where did they go

I can't remember yesterday

But in my mind
I'm a child once more

2009

Mortality

Life can be short, or life can be long,
But one day it will come to its end.

The thing is we won't know
'Til it's over,
But life's been good because I found love,
So I've never been alone.

And I've lived my life
With all the zest I could
So I can say I've done my best
When it's time to rest.

So don't grieve over me; don't weep for me.
I've run my race, now I've flown home.

But forever and always
I'll be living deep within your heart.

I'll be there in your memories
While the clouds roll by,
As the night birds sing,
And as the wind sweeps over my grave.

2009

Sparkie's Song
April 25, 1990–May 23, 2009

I know the time has come
And soon you'll be leaving me

I see the signs

I can see in your eyes you feel it too

Wish I could turn back the time
So this day would never come

But that's how life goes
And I can't hold back the tears
Nor stop my heart from breaking now

So I'll plant a rose for you
Beneath a clear blue sky

Where morning dew
Falls on shining petals
While birds sing this song for you

Then I'll write a symphony
A sweet heartwarming melody
Stemming from memories

That never say good-bye

You'll live on in memories
That never say good-bye

2009

Saying Good-bye

Life's always changing.

One day you're up,
Next day you're down,

Just can't seem to understand
That the simple truth of life is
We are only born to die.

Now all of the years we had
Have suddenly gone away.
Seems like we just said hello;
Now we've said good-bye.

So I have to get through the tears.
I gotta be strong now,
Wake up tomorrow,
And start all over again.

I gotta keep moving,
Gotta keep traveling on,
Just keep on working,
Playing my music loud.

Gotta climb that mountain,
Gotta get to the other side,
Gotta find that river
And cross it before the sun goes down.

Gotta find and cross that river
Before the sun goes down.

2009

LaVergne, TN USA
12 November 2009
163823LV00002BA/81/P